To:

From:

# Tales & Songs of Ireland

RETOLD BY CLAUDINE GANDOLFI

ILLUSTRATED BY JO GERSHMAN

PETER PAUPER PRESS INC.
White Plains, New York

For the dreamer and storyteller in us all

Illustrations copyright © 1999 and 2003 Jo Gershman

Designed by Taryn Sefecka

Copyright © 2003
Peter Pauper Press, Inc.
202 Mamaroneck Avenue
White Plains, NY 10601
All rights reserved
ISBN 0-88088-419-3
Printed in China
7 6 5 4 3 2 1

Visit us at www.peterpauper.com

# Contents

# Introduction

If you've been blessed with the gift of gab, a penchant for spinning a tale, and a rapier-like wit, perhaps you have Irish blood coursing through your veins. There was never a people who treasured story-telling and creativity more than the people of Ireland.

Irish history and legend are filled with remarkable stories that entertain us even as they demonstrate the Irish affinity for paradox. Pagan and Christian beliefs never truly conflicted but melded into a cohesive world-view for the Irish. Though their forebears believed that adhering to the oral tradition kept tales alive through repetition and change, it was the Irish monks who, during the Dark Ages, preserved the past by copying illuminated manuscripts. And it may well be due to their exquisite and painstaking work that the wonderful tales you are about to read are still around today.

C. G.

# The Legend of St. Patrick

No matter what your ancestry, on March 17th everyone is a wee bit Irish. How fitting, then, to learn that St. Patrick, the Patron Saint of Ireland, was an adopted son of Ireland himself! Some claim he was Welsh, others that he was born in Kilpatrick, Scotland, and still others that he was a British Celt. The feast day of St. Patrick, believed to fall on the anniversary of his death, is cause for celebration each year. Oddly, it seems to have greater significance outside of Ireland than within, perhaps due to the desire for those of Irish descent to celebrate their heritage and to share that joyous lineage with the rest of the world. The story of St. Patrick (including the tale of how he drove the snakes from Ireland—a didactic metaphor for Christianity's triumph over pre-Christian paganism) reads like a grand adventure tale, part history, part embellishment, which is perfectly appropriate for the time and people it portrays.

Long before the spread of Christianity in northern Europe, during a time of invasions that followed the dissolution of Roman power, there lived a northern Irish king known as Niall Noigiallach, or Neil of the Nine Hostages. King Niall's men would routinely make raids into the weakened areas of Roman occupation, pirating and plundering what they could, before returning to their kingdom with booty and slaves. One unfortunate captive was a sixteen-year-old lad named Maewyn Succat. Maewyn was well born—a "patrician" to the Romans, which is how he came to be known as "Patrick." He was the son of Calpurnius, who supported his family farm by exercising the duties of *decurio*, or administrator for the Romans. His mother, Conchessa, was a blood relative of St. Martin of Tours—the patron saint of France and of soldiers. Maewyn, whose grandfather was a Christian monk—no vow of chastity was required at the time—was raised in Cumbria. Though not much is known of his childhood, his life from the kidnapping onward has been celebrated for 1600 years through his autobiography, *The Confession of St. Patrick.*

Despite his religious roots, Patrick attributed his descent into slavery

to his lack of faith:

> *I did not know the true God. I was taken into captivity to Ireland*
> *with many thousands of people—and deservedly so, because we turned*
> *away from God, and did not keep His commandments, and did not*
> *obey our priests, who used to remind us of our salvation.*
> From *The Confession of St Patrick,* translated from the Latin by Ludwig Bieler

Once whisked away to the island of Hibernia, as the Romans called Ireland, Patrick was purchased by a farmer from Dalriada and made to tend a herd. During his solitary hours on the farm on Slemish Mountain, Patrick spent most of his time in contemplation, trying to make up for the lack of faith that had lost him everything. During the period of his captivity, he became closer to God. His constant reliance on faith fed his soul as the roots and herbs fed his body, in the pagan land where his beliefs were considered subversive. Motivated by a desire to atone for his sins and filled with the Holy Spirit, Patrick threw himself into his work so that no one could ever say ill of him. He became well liked by the local people.

Laoghaire, son of King Niall, was apprehensive about Patrick. To compound matters, one of the king's druid priests had made a dire prophecy for his reign:

*A man with a shaven head shall come from the west to destroy our gods and seduce our people into becoming his followers. He shall overthrow kings, and his doctrines shall rule forevermore.*

Believing this to mean Patrick, Laoghaire kept a close eye on the captive.

For six years Patrick lived the life of a slave. Though he was a diligent worker, he would make time to say a hundred prayers each day and each night. When he wasn't deep in prayer or busy tending the herd, he was filled with a desire to learn everything there was to know about the people who were his captors. Gaelic became his language, and the Irish customs and religious pantheon the object of his study. Patrick's genuine interest in the Irish inclined them to open up to him. Slowly, he entered into their camaraderie and gained their trust—as much as could be afforded a slave. As the Romans adopted the local customs of each people they conquered,

Patrick would later convert the Irish through his rapport with their culture. As time passed, he made many friends who valued his opinion and companionship. There was a genuine affinity between Patrick and his captors, but still he longed for the day when he could return home to his family and land.

One night while Patrick was sleeping, after a long day tending his flocks, an angel appeared to him in a dream:

"Your penitence has served you well. Soon you shall return home."

Patrick sat up, amazed at the vision. The angel continued:

"Your ship awaits."

Patrick saw in his heart that this was true, and he believed. He escaped from his captors, traveled nearly 200 miles to the sea, and asked the captain of a departing ship to take him home. But the captain saw no purpose or gain for himself in taking Patrick on his boat. Dejected, Patrick started to walk back to the hut where he was hiding, and as he walked, he offered up a prayer. As his prayer ended, one of the sailors on the ship called out to him:

"Wait! If you hurry you can still return to your home. As an act of

faith, you shall be our friend and travel with us. Be our guest in any manner you see fit."

With their assistance, Patrick was able to return home. However, he did not remain long in his birthplace because his life now had gained a new purpose. During the night, another angel—Victoricus—had appeared to him. Patrick sensed that the angel had come to bear a message to him from Ireland. The angel handed him one of countless letters that he carried, called "The Voice of the Irish." As he read, Patrick could hear the voices of that dear people:

"Come back, young man, and live among us once more."

After reading this line, Patrick put the letter away, too broken-hearted to continue. A few nights later, he had another visitation. This time the angel let him know that God was speaking to him, and Patrick became joyful. Determined to devote himself to God and His mission, he decided to travel to France.

Patrick lived in Marmoutier Abbey as a monk, learning Latin and studying for the priesthood. He visited St. Martin's monastery in Tours and frequented places of piety and learning. He became a follower of the

erudite bishop of Auxerre, who would later be known as St. Germain, and who promoted him to full priesthood.

Patrick once again thought of the letter he had received in his dream and wished to be able to fulfill the prophecy. But many church leaders felt that he was unworthy and attempted to discredit him in Rome. Instead of sending Patrick to Ireland, the church appointed St. Palladius to the position of bishop there. Ultimately, after Patrick had proved his worth again and again, the prophecy came true. Palladius was installed as bishop of Scotland and Pope Celestine finally appointed Patrick bishop of the Irish.

Patrick had had a vision of Divine grace that this should come to pass, and that his mission would be to convert his old enemies to Christianity. Thus, 20 years after his escape, he returned to the shores of Ireland, in County Wicklow, with a group of 24 missionaries. He had returned to the Irish at long last, and this time his mission was to bring the people to God.

Knowing that Palladius had failed to establish a strong Christian presence among the Irish because of their resistance to outsiders, Patrick intended to win them over with a combination of a show of strength and his knowledge of their customs. Once he had converted the chieftains, the

masses would follow. Patrick cursed the pagans with one breath and offered Christian blessings with the next.

Upon his arrival, Patrick was besieged by the local king, Nathy. Nathy's attacks had contributed to Palladius's desire to be removed from the Irish see. Once in place, Patrick cursed the king, turning his rich fields into a salty marshland. Patrick and his followers then ventured further into Ireland. This time they were met by Dichu, chieftain in County Down. After a welcome akin to the one he had received from Nathy, Patrick turned the chieftain's attack dog to stone. When Dichu went to retaliate by sword, the offending arm was struck motionless. Dichu, realizing he was no match for Patrick and his God, converted to Christianity on the spot and was immediately healed. Dichu received the teachings of Patrick and in turn granted him a large barn in which to worship—his first church. Later, a monastery would be erected there.

Other stories suggest that Patrick returned to Dalriada and paid Milchu his ransom as a slave. In exchange for this and for past injuries, Milchu converted to Christianity. But Milchu couldn't live with the knowledge of the growing renown of his former slave. He gathered his possessions together

into the family mansion and set the place ablaze, throwing himself on the pyre. One of Milchu's sons eventually joined Patrick as a disciple.

On the pagan feast of Beltane (May 1), when flames were doused so that a symbolic new light might be created from the sun's rays and distributed to all points around the island, the high king rekindled the sacred fire, thereby showing his omnipotence. This flame was passed to his loyal subjects, and on to theirs. Fully aware of the credence the Celts put in the power of their holy day, Patrick staged a defiant coup on Beltane. When the chieftains of Ireland were gathered at Tara, he built a huge bonfire on a nearby hill—knowing full well that the punishment for lighting a fire on Beltane was death.

When the druid priests witnessed the growing flame on the opposing hill, they quickly ran to King Oenghus of Munster with a dire prophecy:

*Extinguish that fire (Christianity) or it will never cease to burn in Ireland!*

At first the king's men attempted to put out the fire, but ultimately the

king chose to hold an audience with Patrick. It was at this meeting that Patrick gave his legendary account of the mystery of the Holy Trinity using a shamrock. The three leaves of the shamrock were the perfect metaphor for God the Father, Son, and Holy Spirit as three beings in one God— each separate, yet each part of a whole. Oenghus converted to Christianity.

Patrick gained many followers and baptized thousands across the land. While baptizing the royal prince, Oenghus, Patrick accidentally leaned on his crosier and pierced Oenghus through the foot. Oenghus endured the pain, thinking it was part of the conversion ritual. When Patrick noticed the spilled blood of the prince, he asked why he had not cried out. Oenghus merely answered that the pain was a small sacrifice for enjoying the blessings of the Christian faith. Pleased with Oenghus's bravery, Patrick etched a cross on the prince's shield with his crosier and promised that this shield would win many victories, both earthly and spiritual.

The legend most closely associated with the saint occurred at Clew Bay. During Lent, Patrick fasted and prayed while perched atop Croagh Patrick, a peak 2,500 feet above sea level. He gathered strength from prayer, and at the end of forty days summoned all the snakes in the

surrounding countryside and cast them into the sea. Symbolically, the serpent was an icon of the druid priests. Patrick casting the serpents from Ireland refers to ridding the country of the old pagan practices, and not to actual snakes—which never managed to cross over the natural land bridge to Ireland before the island was cut off from Scotland during the last ice age.

Patrick was in constant peril as he traveled around the country on his mission. The druid leaders would frequently arrest him, though he always managed to escape. Various miracles were attributed to Patrick, including raising the dead. In this way, Patrick's Christianity was able to rival the magical practices of the druid priests and attract the common people. While some of his converts converted others, others were slain by Britannic chieftains in order to prevent change. Monasteries were established as centers for learning and study. These schools attracted new converts. Christianity spread throughout Ireland and eventually the Irish monks brought the scholarly tradition of Patrick back to mainland Europe, where literacy continued to spread.

Patrick died in his seventies and is allegedly buried in County Down, his mission complete and his prophecy fulfilled. At the cathedral, there is a

slab of stone with "Patric" inscribed on it to signify the burial site. From the moment of his death, the cult of Patrick grew, and within a few hundred years he was worshipped as a saint, long before the Catholic Church established the practice of canonization.

I arise today
Through the strength of heaven:
Light of the sun,
Radiance of the moon,
Splendor of fire,
Speed of lightning,
Swiftness of the wind,
Depth of the sea,
Stability of the earth,
Firmness of rock.

Christ with me, Christ before me, Christ behind me,
Christ within me, Christ beneath me, Christ above me,
Christ on my right, Christ on my left,
Christ when I lie down, Christ when I sit down,
Christ when I arise,
Christ in the heart of every one who thinks of me,
Christ in the mouth of every one who speaks of me,
Christ in every eye that sees me,
Christ in every ear that hears me.

From *St. Patrick's Breast-Plate*, a prayer attributed to Patrick

# The Magical Harp of Dagda

*The harp has become one of the most recognizable symbols of Ireland. Why? Because of the mythical harp possessed by the Dagda, Irish Lord of the Earth, father of all. There are many gifts among his possessions. A cauldron called "Never Dry," blessed with an everlasting supply of nourishment, serves a favorite meal to whoever eats from it. This mystical cauldron refuses sustenance to anyone who does not keep his word, and also to cowards. The Dagda also owns a mighty club that can both slay and revive. But the best known of his triad of magical possessions is his beautiful harp.*

Dagda fought many battles against the Fomorians. The Dagda was the leader of the Tuatha De Danann, a generally fair-haired folk with light colored eyes, while the Fomorians were dark. The Dagda's harp functioned differently in wartime and in peace. During battle, the Dagda would rouse his men into a frenzy with the instrument. Once they returned from the engagement, he'd soothe them with music. The men remembered only the glory of battle, not the pain or suffering. Is it any wonder that Dagda's followers were always ready to fight by his side?

During times of peace, the harp's music magically changed the seasons. It was known as the Harp of the Seasons or Four Cornered Music.

The Fomorians had ruled the land during the reign of Bress and imposed a severe tax on the people. The Dagda spent his time building castles and forts for his livelihood. But once Bress was deposed, war broke out between the Fomorians and the Tuatha De Danann. Though preparations lasted seven years, the Fomorians managed to ready themselves before the Dagda had completed his campaign. Dagda set forth as an ambassador to discuss a delay in the battle. At first it seemed as if he would receive great hospitality from the Fomorians, who offered him a giant banquet of

porridge, which he ate from a hole in the ground. The Dagda took out his great spoon and heartily began his meal, but soon the Fomorians issued a warning: if he could not finish their porridge, they would put him to death. They couldn't have him returning to his people saying they were inhospitable!

Nonplussed, the Dagda managed to eat every last drop of the porridge, scraping the tiniest morsels off the bottom of the hole. He then fell asleep in preparation for battle. This gave the Tuatha De Danann the time they needed to finish their preparations. In the martial encounter that ensued, the Fomorians were defeated—but they did not go without recompense. They managed to sneak into the Dagda's great hall unnoticed during one of the fiercest battles. They found the harp hanging in its place of honor and promptly made off with it. Knowing that the harp was of great value, they fled as fast as they could, riding for many miles across the land and stopping only when they had reached safety. An unoccupied castle was found, and the Fomorian chieftains arranged for a banquet, placing the purloined harp on the wall as a war prize for all to see.

Unbeknownst to them, the Dagda sensed the harp's theft and followed

the Fomorian raiders to their hiding place. In the midst of their celebration, the main doors to the banquet hall burst open and the Dagda appeared with several of his men. Before the Fomorian chieftains could get to their weapons, the Dagda summoned his harp. From its place on the wall, the harp sailed across the banquet hall into the Dagda's arms, smashing through anyone who tried to get in its way.

Reunited with its rightful owner, the harp became a powerful ally. The Dagda's fingers sounded three chords, and the Music of Tears issued forth from the harp. The keening melody swept across the great hall. Women sobbed, little children cried, and the strong warriors of Fomor turned their heads so no one would see them weeping. Once more the Dagda strummed the strings. This time the Music of Mirth filled the air. The Fomorians were struck with laughter, gentle at first, then growing stronger, so that soon every warrior was doubled over in a raucous fit of the giggles so potent they could no longer hold their weapons. The Dagda played his harp a third time, and the Music of Sleep overtook the Fomorians. Sweet and gentle dreams soon filled the formerly angry hall. Mothers held their babes in their laps, the elderly nodded off, and the warriors closed their eyes and drifted

off to dreamland.

The Dagda stood at the entranceway to the hall and surveyed the magic the harp had made. Smiling, he turned with his men and left the Fomorians to their peaceful sleep, choosing to return to his own homecoming.

The Dagda became the king of the Tuatha De Danann and allocated underground dwellings to each of his relations so that they would never leave their homeland. These people eventually become known as the sidhe, or fairy folk, and this is one of the legends of their origin. Dagda is said to be buried near the Boyne River.

# The Wooing of Etain

*The fantastical world of the Irish has room for more flights of fancy than any other canon of legend. In this tale, Oenghus (Angus), the God of Love, acts as divine savior for poor Etain, whose life—or lives, as the case may be—is filled with turbulent twists. The theme of forbidden love between mortal and god illuminates the prevailing force of love as well as man's far-reaching ambition. Etain is the unattainable beauty who draws people to her. She possesses an open heart and a caring soul—as well as an iron will.*

The god Midir, brother of Oenghus, fell madly in love with a mortal woman named Etain, daughter of Ailill of Echraidhe. Etain's beauty was of such renown that to refer to a woman as "fair as Etain" was the highest compliment. In order to win Etain for Midir, Oenghus was required to perform three fantastical tasks for Ailill.

Then Ailill gave her over in marriage. There was, however, an additional obstacle to be overcome—Midir's first wife, Fuamnach. Jealous of Etain, Fuamnach had the mortal woman transformed into a pool of water, then a worm, and finally a purple butterfly.

Even in her altered state, Etain was, because of her association with Midir, blessed with magical powers. She had the ability to hum Midir to sleep and also to warn him of an enemy's approach. Fuamnach was still jealous and sent a powerful wind to carry the butterfly Etain far away from Midir. Etain was swept away into Oenghus's palace. Oenghus constructed a beautiful bower for her, filled with the sweetest flowers, and she lived there for seven years. Oenghus countered Fuamnach's spell by allowing Etain to regain human form during the night hours that she spent with him. But before Oenghus could summon Midir, Fuamnach sent another wind that blew Etain to the far edges of Ireland. There Etain was condemned to flutter in the wilderness for a thousand years.

On a certain day, the butterfly fell into a goblet of wine being sipped by the wife of King Etar of Echrad, hero of Ulster, and was swallowed. Rather than being digested, Etain was transformed into the female child to

whom Etar's wife subsequently gave birth. When Midir found out what had happened, he went to seek his love, undaunted by the passage of a millennium.

Meanwhile, the king of Ireland, Eochaid (Yo-hee) Airem, held a grand feast at Tara. Newly ascended to the throne, Eochaid proclaimed that he would need a wife. She could not be a mere woman—she must possess extraordinary qualities that would make her fit to be the queen of all Ireland. King Eochaid's men scoured the land for a maiden of noble birth blessed with unsurpassed beauty and grace. They found the perfect woman in Etain, the daughter of King Etar.

King Eochaid journeyed through the meadows of Bri Leith, and there he chanced upon a maiden preparing to wash her cascades of golden hair in the clear water. Her garments were made of fine green silk, and her cloak was of the deepest purple. She held a silver comb embossed in gold, echoing the four golden birds adorning her basin. As the king approached, he was captivated by her delicate skin and eyes of hyacinth blue. She was undoubtedly the most beautiful woman he had ever encountered. The king was sure that this must be Etain, the fairest woman in all the land.

"Who are you, fair maiden, and where are you from?" queried the king.

"Those are easy questions to answer. I am Etain, daughter of the king of Echrad of the fairy-mound."

The king smiled. He had found his future bride. "May I request an hour's dalliance with you?"

"That was my intention when you summoned me," she said coyly. "I have lived here for twenty years, dwelling on the fairy-mound. Nobles, kings, and all manner of men have come to court me. But I have been waiting for you, my King. I have loved you since I was but a small child, unable to speak. Although I have never seen you or heard your name, I recognized you at once."

"That is the best invitation I have ever received," said Eochaid. "I shall make you welcome, and all other women shall I leave for your sake. I shall live together with you for as long as you will have me." A bride-price of seven bond slaves was given to Etain, and she journeyed with Eochaid to Tara, where the king's jubilant hospitality was enjoyed by all.

The three sons of Finn—King Eochaid Airem, Eochaid Fedlech, and Ailill Anglonnach—feasted at Tara. It was there that Ailill fell in love with

the unsurpassed Etain. Ailill's wife noticed her husband's gaze following the golden-haired beauty and questioned him about it. He grew embarrassed and could not look at Etain. After the month-long celebration at Tara, Ailill traveled to his brother's stronghold at Dun Fremain. It was at Dun Fremain that he began pining for Etain. He spent a year growing weak with lovesickness, but he would not speak of his love to anyone. King Eochaid knew that something was troubling his brother deeply.

"How goes it with you, Ailill? You seem ill, yet it cannot be anything very serious, since you have been this way for quite some time, unchanged."

"Surely I grow worse both day and night!"

"What ails you?"

"Truly, I wish I knew."

Concerned for his weary brother, Eochaid called for the royal doctor. Upon examining the patient, the learned man offered two possible causes for Ailill's illness: he was either sick with jealousy or smitten with unrequited love. His secret discovered, Ailill grew ashamed but would not confirm the cause of his malady.

As fate would have it, King Eochaid now began his royal circuit throughout Ireland. He left Etain at Dun Fremain to care for his brother. She was to treat him gently and kindly as long as he lived. Should he die, the king left specific instructions for his burial. He did not expect his brother to live to see his return at the end of the circuit.

Etain visited her brother-in-law each day as her husband had instructed. She tended to him, sang to him, and made sure he had all possible comforts. Finally, she confronted him.

"What is the matter, Ailill? Your sickness is so great that we are all concerned. If there is anything we can do to help you recover, we will do it without hesitation." Ailill thought carefully, and at last he gave her an answer. . . .

Etain continued to visit Ailill each day and she helped him greatly. She wasted no time and spared no expense, knowing as she did that she was the cause of his affliction. Although she did not love him, she could not bear seeing him in such a miserable way. Finally, she told Ailill that she would tryst with him in the house outside the king's stronghold and grant his every desire. Alive with anticipation, Ailill could not sleep the entire

night. But as the time for their meeting grew near, he became tired and unwillingly fell into a deep sleep.

Etain waited for Ailill at the appointed place. There she saw a man approaching who had Ailill's countenance, but she knew it was not he. When Ailill awoke he was wracked with anguish. He had missed the trysting time! He was thinking he would rather die than live, when Etain arrived at his door and promised to meet him at the same place on the next day. But, the next day the same fate befell Ailill, and the same man appeared to Etain.

"You are not the man I have come to meet. Who are you and why are you here?"

"It was fitting for you to tryst with me when you were the daughter of King Ailill of Echraidhe. I was your first husband."

"What is your name? I demand it of you."

"It has never been hard to answer to you, Etain. Midir of Bri Leith is what I am called."

"And why did you part from me if you are who you claim to be?"

"Again, it is with pleasure that I answer these questions for you. The

spells of Fuamnach tore us apart." Midir took Etain's hand. "Will you come with me?"

She pulled away from his grasp, "No! I will not trade the king of Ireland for the likes of you, a man of whose lineage and family I know nothing."

Midir smiled, "It was I who filled the heart of Ailill with longing for you. I also prevented him from keeping your assignation. I will not allow him to ruin your honor." Midir turned and left Etain in the house by the stronghold.

A confused Etain visited with Ailill. She told him of the man she had met. His reaction only confirmed what Midir had told her. Ailill was cured of the wasting sickness. He was overjoyed that he was no longer ill and that he had not caused Etain to be unfaithful, and he blessed Etain and the stranger. Etain and Ailill agreed that it was fortunate that everything had turned out as it did.

When the king returned from his trek, he asked after his brother and was told the entire tale. He agreed that it was a blessing that things had happened as they did. Later, while out on his lands, the king happened to

meet a young warrior who held a five-pointed spear in one hand and a gem-encrusted shield in the other. He was dressed in the finest garments. His blonde hair hung down to his shoulders and his eyes were a clear gray. The king did not know him, but the warrior immediately placed himself under the king's protection.

"Welcome to my kingdom, unknown hero."

"Ah, your hospitality is just as I expected it to be. Thank you."

"I am not familiar with your likeness."

"But I know you well!" the stranger laughed.

"What are you called?" asked the impatient king.

"I am not well known. But if you must know it, I am Midir of Bri Leith."

"And for what reason have you journeyed here?" asked the king.

"Why, to play a game of chess with you, of course."

The king brightened, "I am highly skilled at chess."

"And I am here to test that skill."

"Unfortunately, young man, the chess board is stored in the queen's apartments, and she has not yet risen today."

But Midir came prepared. "I have with me a chessboard that rivals your own. There is no need to bother your queen." At that, Midir revealed an ornate silver chessboard encrusted with precious stones and gold playing pieces, which he carried in a pouch of brass chain mail.

"I will not start to play until we have decided upon a stake," said the king.

"What prize do you wish to play for?"

"It matters not to me, sir."

"Very well," answered Midir. "If you win, I will give you fifty gray horses of the finest quality."

Midir went on describing the valuable trophies that he would wager, but the king wanted none of it. He preferred the prize to be something that would benefit his entire kingdom. He asked that Midir's people clear away the rocks from the plains and remove the rushes around the stronghold. He further desired them to cut down the forest of Breg and build a bridge across the moor of Lamrach to allow men to pass freely across it.

Midir agreed to all of this. He then played and lost a game of chess to the king. And so it was that Midir and his fairy host carried out King

Eochaid's will. The king noticed that Midir's fairy folk did not harness their oxen with straps over their brows but used wooden yokes. And so it happened that King Eochaid came to be known as Eochaid the Plowman, and he spread the use of this method of plowing throughout Ireland. Midir's forces toiled for Eochaid. Each task put before them was completed in a timely manner and was done exceedingly well.

But there was a breach caused by the fairy folk. Midir caught a steward of the king complaining about one of the fairy workers. Midir, angered at the disparaging talk, went to speak with the king, who welcomed him again.

"Your welcome is what I fully expected. There is nothing that you asked that has not been done. But now I am angered with you."

"I do not harbor any ill will toward you, Midir. What is your wish? I shall make it so."

"As you say," thought Midir. "Shall we play at chess again?" he asked.

"What stakes shall we choose this time?"

"Whatever the winner asks," said Midir, who proceeded to trounce the king swiftly.

"My stake is forfeit to you," said the king.

"If I had wished it, it would have been forfeited long ago."

"What is it that you wish?"

"That I hold Etain in my arms and steal a kiss from her!"

The king fell silent, knowing he had to grant this request. He asked Midir to return in one month's time to collect his winnings. The king did not know that Midir had been wooing Etain in secret. Though Midir called her the Fair-haired Woman, she would not come with him. Etain insisted that the king grant permission for her to accompany Midir back to his home in the fairy world. And so Midir deliberately lost the original chess game in order to win the forfeiture of the second. Everything had gone according to plan.

Because he respected the might of the legions of Midir, the king summoned his best men to protect his stronghold. All the champions of Ireland were stationed inside Tara. Eochaid's fortress had never before been so well defended. Windows were shut tight, doors were locked. As Etain was dispensing wine to his men, Midir appeared in the middle of the banquet hall, to the amazement of the assembled crowd. The king greeted him hastily

and gave him welcome.

"This is how I expected you would greet me, King Eochaid," said Midir. "Now let me have what you have promised me. The debt is due. I have given you everything you asked for; now you must respond in kind."

"I have not yet thought over your request, Midir."

"You have promised me Etain on this day. I have your word."

Etain blushed in her shame.

"Do not blush," said Midir to Etain. "You have in no way dishonored yourself. I have pursued you for well over a year, plying you with the best gems that Ireland can offer, and yet I have not touched you. It is not through your actions that I have won you."

"I have told you," said Etain. "Until Eochaid willingly grants me to you, I will not go with you. If he does not agree, I shall grant you nothing."

"And I do not grant you to him," said the king. "But he shall take you in his arms anyway!"

"And so I shall," shouted Midir.

As he uttered these words, Midir and Etain were transformed into a pair of swans and flew from the palace at Tara. The king scoured the land

and destroyed the fairy-mounds, one by one, until he chanced upon the mound at Bri Leith. From within, Midir sent forth sixty women, all with the visage of Etain. No one could tell which was the true queen; even Eochaid was deceived.

Finally, he chose Mess Buachalla, Etain's daughter, instead of his own queen. When he realized his mistake, he returned to Bri Leith and plundered it. Etain at last gave a sign to make herself known to Eochaid and he bore her away to Tara in triumph.

# Oenghus and Caer

*In the lore of Irish mythology, no one figure did more to ensure that the course of true love ran smoothly than Oenghus Mac Oc. Oenghus, the God of Love, is described as being followed by four birds, who represent his kisses and symbolize his divinity. Avian imagery runs through the tales in which Oenghus appears. He uses his powers to assist lovers, especially those facing impossible odds, like Midir in the tale of the wooing of Etain. This is the story of Oenghus's own quest for love.*

O enghus had been surrounded by magic, even at birth. The god known as the Dagda and the goddess Boann concealed their illicit union and Boann's pregnancy by causing the earth to cease revolving around the sun for nine months. This trick caused Oenghus to be conceived and born on the same day. Because of these unusual circumstances,

Oenghus was infused with the power of the sun and grew into a wondrous young man who shone with the spirit of innocence, love, and virtue.

Thoughts of love preoccupied young Oenghus's mind, but none so touched him as one that appeared to him in a dream. For a year, Oenghus dreamt of a woman whom he did not know. She was astonishingly beautiful—as dream lovers tend to be. Each night she would beckon him, but before he could reach her, she would disappear. Oenghus knew he could love only this mysterious woman and accept only her as his wife. So obsessed was Oenghus with his dream maiden that he gradually grew more and more distracted from everyday life. All around him noticed that he was listless, pale, and increasingly weak.

Physicians tried to determine the cause of Oenghus's wasting sickness. Though Oenghus knew the cause, he would not disclose it. He feared ridicule if it should become known that the great Oenghus had been struck weak by a dream of a woman who had no earthly or heavenly form. At long last, Fergne—the best physician in the land—proclaimed that Oenghus was lovesick.

Boann the River Goddess set off on a quest to find the maiden who

had appeared to her son. Such a maiden had to exist; the determined Boann would find her. But her quest took too long for the Dagda, who set off on a search of his own. Neither was successful. Boann summoned her brother, Bobd Dearg, to help find the woman from Oenghus's dream. Bobd Dearg combed the countryside for a year in search of the dream maiden.

Bobd Dearg finally returned with news. The woman in question existed in flesh and blood. She lived at a lake in Connacht, a known portal to the otherworld; her father was a Dannan god. Finally, Oenghus learned her name: Caer Ibormeith, which means yew-berry. Energized by the news, Oenghus traveled to the castle of King Ailill and Queen Maeve of Connacht. With intervention from the Dagda, King Ailill and Oenghus tried to set up a meeting with Caer's father, Ethal. However, Ethal refused to meet with them. King Ailill was angered by Ethal's refusal and sent his soldiers to destroy the fairy-mound where Ethal lived. Ethal would not be forced. He staunchly refused to hand over his daughter to the likes of King Ailill, knowing as he did that her marriage foretold his own death. Ethal made it clear that his daughter's powers were greater than his: there was fairy magic involved. A show of force would never win her hand. Oenghus

would have to find Caer and ask her to marry him. The decision to go with him, or not to, would be hers alone.

Oenghus soon learned that the maiden he loved lived on Loch Bel Dragon, the Lake of the Dragon's Mouth, with one hundred and fifty other damsels. Caer was a shape-shifter. For every year she spent as a human, she was obliged to spend another in the form of a swan. Oenghus pleaded with Ethal, who finally told him that if Oenghus truly loved Caer, he must meet her at the lake during the feast of Samhain (SOW-in). During that holiday, the link between worlds was stretched thin; Oenghus might be able to woo her away.

On the appointed date, Oenghus made his way to the lake in Connacht, where he came upon a beautiful vision. The light danced across the swan-laden water, reflected on the silver necklaces of one hundred and fifty swans. The necklaces joined each pair of swans together at their long, silky necks. Caer's alone was made of gold and shone the brightest. Oenghus beckoned to her.

"Caer! Caer! Please come to me!"

"Who calls?" she replied.

"It is I, Oenghus Mac Oc, and I have loved you in my dreams. I die for love of you."

Hearing his pleas, Caer replied that she would agree to meet with him only in the form of a swan. She would not relinquish her shape-shifting powers for anyone. Oenghus agreed. Invoking the power of his love, he turned the cloak that he wore into wings of the purest white feathers and joined her in swan form on the lake. The couple embraced. Three times they glided across the lake, singing in unison. Their song was so beautiful that all who heard it were lulled to sleep for three days.

After they were mated, the swans flew to Oenghus's home, Brugh na Bóinne, in Newgrange. Returning to human form, they threw a grand celebration feast for all the land. There was great joy and merrymaking on that day, and happiness reigned ever after.

# Diarmaid and Grainne

*Fionn MacCumhail, or Finn MacCool, the hero of the Fianna, is the wronged husband in this tale of adulterous love between Diarmaid and Grainne. Grainne, though under the influence of fairy magic, is not the steadfast heroine of the Irish that is Deirdre of the Sorrows. She is full of fears and desires, and is drawn to the primitive side of life. Oenghus, the God of Love, intercedes on behalf of these lovers to act as their protector. As in many Irish legends,* Diarmaid and Grainne *features characters who were once human. The occurrence of shape-shifting in Irish tales signals a belief in the immortality of the soul. Often, death is not the cessation of life but merely a change. The Irish mirrored this philosophy in their decorative knotwork, whose patterns had neither beginning nor end.*

Though mortal, Diarmaid Ua Duibhne had Oenghus the God of Love as foster father. He grew up at Oenghus's home at Newgrange and became one of the most famed heroes of the Fianna. Early in his life, Diarmaid encountered a fairy woman who touched his brow with her finger, leaving him with a love-spot. No woman who saw that spot could resist him.

Fionn MacCumhail, the aging champion of the Fianna, had decided to marry. He chose the High King's daughter, Grainne. A great betrothal feast was held and many of the Fianna attended, including Diarmaid. Grainne, however, did not wish to marry the older hero. She wanted a young husband and began seeking a savior among the gathered guests. Through a stroke of luck, the hat that Diarmaid wore to cover his love-spot fell off, and Grainne fell immediately under the enchantment of Diarmaid.

Determined to win him, the quick-thinking Grainne drugged the guests with a sleeping potion before the ceremony could take place, and placed a *geis*—a request that could not be refused by a warrior without loss of honor—upon Diarmaid. Her geis was that Diarmaid should elope with her. Caught between the wrath of Fionn and the loss of his honor,

Diarmaid accepted the geis, but with two conditions: during their elopement, Grainne must neither mount on horseback nor travel by foot, and she must greet him neither indoors nor outdoors. Not to be deterred, Grainne met Diarmaid the following day on a billygoat standing at the threshold of the keep. His conditions met, Diarmaid agreed to elope with her, but he refused to become her lover.

When Fionn became aware of Grainne's deception, he grew enraged. For sixteen years he chased the couple relentlessly. As he neglected his duties as leader, Ireland fell into disrepair and near anarchy. Through his magical insight, Fionn was able to locate the couple repeatedly, but thanks to Diarmaid's foster father, Oenghus, they always escaped. Eventually, Grainne's deepest wish was fulfilled, and the pair became lovers.

At long last, Fionn tracked the pair to Oenghus's stronghold at Newgrange. Unwilling to allow a battle, Oenghus proposed a truce between the two. They agreed. Diarmaid was finally welcomed as the king's son-in-law and Fionn married another of the High King's beautiful daughters. Fionn, however, never forgot the pain that Diarmaid had caused him. . . .

One day, Fionn's men arranged a hunt for the great boar of Ben

Bulben. This was no ordinary boar. Born as the human son of Diarmaid's mother and Oenghus's steward, Roc, the offspring was killed by Oenghus's father, probably in revenge for Diarmaid's mother's infidelity. Roc could not bear the death of his son and so he turned him into a mighty boar without hair, ears, or tail. This boar, he decreed, would some day kill Diarmaid—the death of one son for another.

Diarmaid knew nothing of his misbegotten half-brother until Fionn's invitation to the hunt. Fionn related the history of the beast, and Diarmaid realized Fionn had lured him into a trap. But Diarmaid was not one to shirk his responsibilities. If he was fated to die here, he would. During the hunt, he was disemboweled by the boar as he dealt it a death blow.

The mortally wounded Diarmaid begged for assistance from Fionn. There was one thing that could cure Diarmaid—a drink from the hands of Fionn. The hero of the Fianna brought back a handful of water for Diarmaid three times. But each time Fionn remembered what had happened between them and let the life-saving drink trickle through his fingers.

Diarmaid died, and his body was brought to Oenghus's stronghold in Newgrange. So distraught was Oenghus that he sent a soul into Diarmaid's

lifeless body each day so that he might continue to talk with his son. Unfortunately, the resurrection lasted for only a few moments each day. Knowing that she could no longer be with Diarmaid, Grainne at first fought against Fionn, calling upon her sons to exact revenge. When this proved futile, she arranged to meet with Fionn personally. Grainne met with Fionn a second and then a third time, and on the fourth meeting, the two decided to make peace. They wed a short time later.

# Songs of Ireland

PERFORMED BY
THE NEW MILLENNIUM CHORUS AND SYMPHONY ORCHESTRA

Track 1 • *Legacy* (4:36)

Track 2 • *A Ghaoth Andeas* (4:36)

Track 3 • *Emerald Pride* (5:33)

Track 4 • *Liam O Raghallaigh* (5:04)

Track 5 • *Banchnoic Eireann O* (5:04)

Track 6 • *A Stor, A Stor, A Ghra* (4:17)

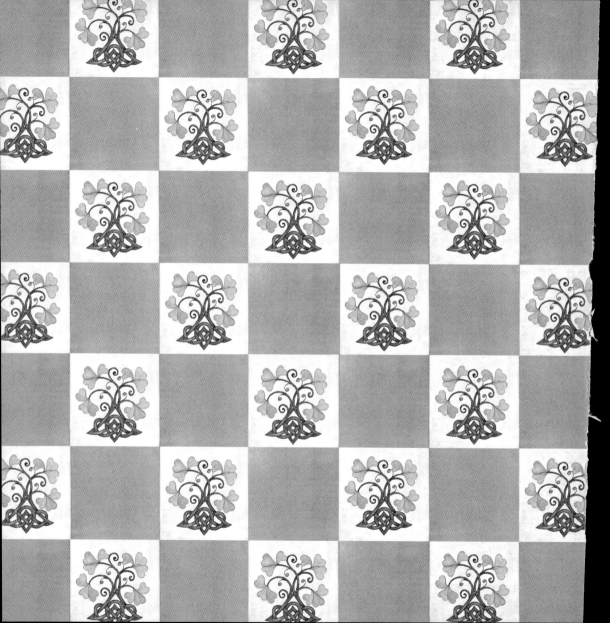